Early Egyptians

George Hart

Sampson Low

General Editor:
Eric Inglefield

Editor:
Jan Burgess

Designer:
Jacky Cowdrey

Picture Researchers:
Anne-Marie Ehrlich
Kathy Brandt

Illustrators:
Eddie Brockwell
Jeff Burns
Dick Eastland
Ron Embleton
Dan Escott
Bryan Evans/Temple
Art Agency
Liz Graham-Yooll
Richard Hook
Angus McBride
John Sibbick

© 1979 Theorem Publishing Ltd
Produced by Theorem Publishing
Ltd, 71-73 Gt Portland Street,
London W1N 5DH.
Published in 1979 by
Sampson Low,
Berkshire House, Queen Street,
Maidenhead, Berkshire SL6 1NF.
Made and printed by
Purnell & Sons Ltd,
Paulton, Avon
SBN 562 00123 9

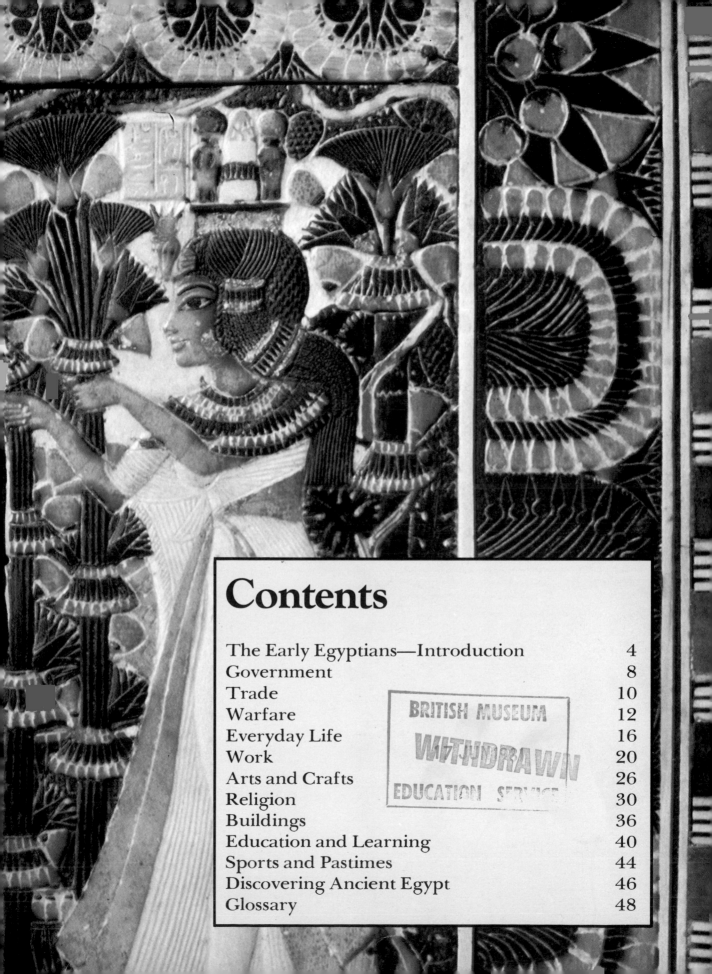

Contents

The Early Egyptians

The Ancient Egyptians were descended from many different tribes and races. In early times, nomads from the desert east of the River Nile and from Palestine settled in the fertile land of Egypt, while Libyan tribes crossed westwards into the Nile Delta and oases of the desert. Even traders from Mesopotamia and South-eastern Iran made the long journey by sea to Egypt.

Africans from the Sudan married into the families of people living in southern Egypt. With such a mix of peoples, it is not surprising that the Egyptians had a colourful culture and complex beliefs. Also, because Egypt stretched about 1,200 kilometres along the banks of the Nile, from its natural frontier at the Aswan cataract, to the Mediterranean coast, speech and customs varied greatly.

For people living in Egypt, the river Nile was a life-line. It rises in the lakes of Uganda and the mountains of Ethiopia, and cuts its way northwards to the sea. The Egyptians always lived along the banks of the Nile as it provided most of the arable soil in a land which otherwise consisted almost totally of desert.

Every year the Nile used to overflow its banks and flood the countryside. The Egyptians thought that this was caused by Hapy, god of the Nile. In fact, it happened because rain in Central Africa and melting snow in Ethiopia increased the amount of water in the river and its tributaries. The flood-waters of the Nile carried rich mud or silt that was then deposited in a layer over the land when the river receded. The

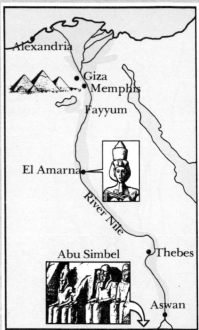

Towns and villages were built along the banks of the Nile. Boats made of papyrus stalks were a common form of transport, while on land, donkeys were used as pack animals. Children often tended livestock while men irrigated the fields. Each town built a shrine to its local god, as the jackal-worshippers have done here.

A striking feature of the Nile valley is the sudden change from fertile ground into desert. Farmers used all arable soil for crops, so large stone monuments were built beyond the fields.

Egyptians used this fertile silt for growing their crops and even called their country *Kemi*, the Black Land.

Egyptian farmers based their calendar on the Nile's flood, dividing the year into three seasons, 'Flooding', 'Growth' and 'Harvest' which each lasted four months. Careful use of water fed by canals into the fields would produce a second harvest. The reputation of Egypt as a gigantic granary spread across the ancient world. The Nile, however, was unpredictable. An extra-high flood could sweep away the huts of the villagers and drown livestock, while a low flood brought too little silt causing crop failure and famine.

In very early times, the Nile entered the sea much further south. Gradually, layers of silt built up at the river mouth creating a fertile region. Because of its resemblance to the triangular Greek capital letter D this region was called the Delta. In ancient Egypt there were seven branches of the Nile flowing into the sea and the whole area was criss-crossed by canals. This wide, marshy delta was called Lower Egypt and it contrasted strongly with the narrow strip of the Nile Valley which was known as Upper Egypt. The Egyptians looked on the deserts as appendages to Egypt proper. In the Western

Desert, people had settled near the oases and sent produce along the caravan routes into the Nile Valley. The arid Eastern Desert was abundant in minerals that the Egyptians mined.

For a long time, Egypt was split into two kingdoms, one in the north and the other in the south. The Ancient Egyptian state came into being in about 3,100 B.C. when Narmer, the ruler of the southerners, conquered the northern kingdom. Even after the two countries were joined under one king, or 'pharaoh', the people still regarded the north and south as two distinct political regions. Recognizing this, the pharaoh called himself 'Lord of the Two Lands'. He moved his capital north to Memphis which was a fortress-city specially founded to rule both parts of Egypt. As a result, the city of Memphis was known as 'the balance of the two lands'.

The Egyptians did not record their history systematically, but Egyptologists have discovered much about the life and events of Ancient Egypt. Occasionally, a king's reign was commemorated in yearly records that stressed important occurrences such as the building of a temple or the conquest of a foreign tribe. Some historical facts were included in the sometimes pompous inscriptions carved by pharaohs to glorify their victories, or disguise their defeats!

It was not until the third century B.C. that an Egyptian priest called Manetho attempted to write a proper history of Egypt. He divided it into 'dynasties' or successive ruling families, and listed 31 dynasties down to the conquest of Egypt by Alexander the Great in 323 B.C. Modern Egyptologists group these dynasties together into various longer periods of history called the Old Kingdom, which was the time when the famous pyramids were built, the Middle Kingdom when centralized government reached its peak, and the New Kingdom when Egyptian influence and power was at its height.

Right: The pharaoh's regalia was intended to convince his people that he was an unconquerable ruler. The three crowns symbolized his political power. The White Crown indicated his rule over southern Egypt and the Red Crown his rule over northern Egypt. The combined crowns represented Egypt united.

White Crown

Red Crown

Combined Crown

Archaic Period
Dynasties 1-2
3,100-2,686 B.C.
Narmer welded north and south Egypt into one kingdom.

Old Kingdom
Dynasties 3-6
2,686-2,181 B.C. The Egyptians built the world's first huge stone monument.

Middle Kingdom
Dynasties 11-12
2,133-1,786 B.C.
Massive forts were built to protect trade on the Nile.

New Kingdom
Dynasties 18-20
1,567-1,085 B.C.
Warrior pharaohs conquered parts of the Middle East.

Ancient Egypt was born over 5,000 years ago, when Narmer, the ruler of southern Egypt, led his troops to fight against the northern king. Narmer clubbed the enemy king to death and captured his towns. He then sailed round the Delta, beheading any opponents, and took control of all Egypt. His beard and tall crown became symbols of royalty for all the pharaohs who followed him.

Some other terms which Egyptologists often use are the Archaic Period which refers to the time when the state of Egypt was very young; the Hyksos Period which refers to the time when the government of Egypt fell into the hands of Bedouin chiefs; and the Ptolemaic Period when the descendants of Ptolemy, who was Alexander the Great's general, ruled the country.

When the Egyptian queen Cleopatra committed suicide in 30 B.C., Egypt became one of the provinces of Rome. Later, Christianity gradually spread through the Nile Valley, eroding the culture and beliefs of the early Egyptians. Finally, in the seventh century A.D., the spread of Islam turned Egypt into the Arab country that it is today.

Late Period
Dynasties 21-30
1,085-343 B.C.
Theban priests ruled the south and a strong Delta family ruled the north.

Ptolemaic Period
332-30 B.C.
Alexander the Great conquered Egypt and Greek pharaohs ruled the country.

The End of Ancient Egypt
30 B.C.-A.D. 641
Egypt became a Roman province. Christianity spread. Arabs and Islam conquered Egypt.

Egyptian history was first divided into dynasties over 2,000 years ago. Egyptologists still refer to these dynasties but group them together to make up larger periods of time. Major groups form 'Kingdoms'. Information about Ancient Egypt has come down to us from royal texts, officials' tombs, letters from foreign rulers and, of course, archaeological finds.

Government

In Ancient Egypt, the head of the state was the pharaoh, who was believed to be both a super-human and a god. He was the living emblem of the god Horus whom the other gods had made the ruler of Egypt. At his coronation the king took five 'great names' symbolizing his political and religious power. On the front of his crown he always wore the symbol of his authority, the cobra-goddess Wadjet who was thought to spit fire at the pharaoh's enemies. The straight, false beard he wore was a ceremonial reminder of the short beards of the earliest rulers. His sceptres were the stylised whip and the crook, which symbolized his leadership.

The pharaoh's word was the law. He governed his people according to the rules of the universe which the Egyptians thought the sun-god had laid down at the time of the creation of the world.

Many kings governed Egypt well, but if a pharaoh issued decrees that damaged the economy or upset traditional ways of life, his successor could always reverse them. Occasionally there were periods of anarchy. For example, King Sethnakht came to the throne when there had been a famine, murder among high officials, and widespread stealing. Sometimes political intrigue in the pharaoh's palace led to assassination plots.

The queen played an important part in the government of Egypt. Although the pharaoh possessed a harem of ladies, he had one 'Great Royal Wife', who was usually of royal birth, and who bore the future heirs. Her son would become the prince that the reigning pharaoh would make his co-regent, and train in statecraft. The queen was frequently a forceful influence in policy-making. Occasionally, when there were no royal sons, a queen ruled Egypt by herself but this form of government was not usually successful, normally lasting only a few years.

Below the pharaoh, the highest official in the land was the vizier, chief executive of all Egypt. The vizier administered the law as impartially as possible and was overlord of the treasury. A multitude of bureaucrats carried out the commands of the higher officials. These bureaucrats belonged to the educated class of 'scribes'. They often had to sail the length of Egypt collecting taxes for the government and, in remote areas, had to have armed escorts to enforce their authority. They would also deal out punishment for failure to pay the tributes of crops or cattle due to the pharaoh. Usually this meant a vigorous beating with canes. More serious crimes were sometimes punished with deep knife cuts in the flesh which served as a permanent reminder.

There was a police force known as the *medjay*, but it was more concerned with dealing out punishment than detective work. Nubians were hired to serve as policemen because they were particularly tall and strong. The administrative centre

Beneath the pharaoh, the Egyptian people were divided into a system of ranks. Ordinary working people at the bottom laboured to support the elite classes at the top. Fieldworkers tended the crops. Above them, craftsmen made furniture and jewellery, and musicians and dancers entertained the upper classes. Higher up were the educated class of scribes.

Above: Petty crimes were usually punished by a quick beating. Scribes ordered canings for men who failed to pay their taxes. Traitors or tomb-robbers were tortured and executed. Other criminals could have their ears or noses cut off. Convicts were sometimes made to work in mines or man frontier-posts.
Left: A painted limestone head of Queen Nefertiti. During this period (Dynasty XVIII) queens were especially powerful. Nefertiti married the pharaoh Akhenaten and helped him put his ideas on sun worship into practice.

and record office for Egypt was at Memphis for most of the time, but later Memphis lost some of its importance to the new city of Alexandria on the Mediterranean coast.

Below the status of scribes, ordinary people were conscripted by the state to perform manual labour, unless specifically excluded by royal decree. For example field-workers were unemployed when the Nile was in flood. So, for three or four months a year, they were organized into gangs of labourers to help build huge stone monuments, such as the pyramids, for the pharaohs, or temples for the gods. Men were also put to work digging and repairing the large network of irrigation canals under the supervision of officials. This national service was an essential part of Egypt's economy.

Trade

Trade between Egypt and the countries of the Middle East began in the earliest times. Trade abroad was the concern of the pharaoh and private bartering was restricted to transactions inside Egypt. The pharaoh commissioned officials to visit foreign countries and exchange goods. Foreign trading missions presented their goods at the Egyptian court. Often such commerce was described by the Egyptians as 'tribute' to the pharaoh because it flattered the pharaoh's sense of importance and removed any notion of the pharaoh being involved in sordid haggling over prices.

Paintings in tombs give an excellent picture of the trade conducted by Egypt. Cretans met Egyptians at the port of Byblos in the Lebanon and exchanged such goods as bolts of cloth, perfume containers sometimes shaped like a rooster's or a bull's head, and metal ingots from which the Egyptians manufactured statuettes. Middle Eastern merchants brought luxury goods like decorated gold vases inlaid with semi-precious stones. They also supplied silver, as the Egyptians had none in their country; horses for chariots; and animals with a rarity value such as the Syrian bear or Indian elephant. From the Lebanon the Egyptians imported cedar logs for building as good-quality wood was scarce along the Nile. From equatorial Africa came incense, leopard skins, ostrich eggs, feathers for fans, and ebony and ivory for ornaments and inlays for furniture. In exchange, Egypt could offer gold from mines in the Eastern Desert, linen, jewellery and grain.

One famous trading expedition was sent by Queen Hatshepsut to the land of Punt (present-day Somalia) and she proudly recorded it on the walls of her temple at Deir el-Bahari in Thebes. The Queen's five boats sailed along the Red Sea coast to Punt. The Egyptians found it a woody and marshy land where people lived in huts on stilts.

The Egyptians traded for incense-bearing trees which Hatshepsut wanted to decorate her monuments. The gum-resin they bore could also be used in temple ceremonies. The Egyptian boats were loaded up with the trees and a cargo of baboons and monkeys.

The large trading vessels of Queen Hatshepsut unload their cargoes from Somalia on the Nile's banks. The incense trees will be planted in the forecourt of the Queen's temple at Thebes. Elephants' tusks will be made into furniture or perfume containers. The leopard might be kept at court as a royal pet. The baboons climbing in the rigging are sacred animals.

R Phillips 78

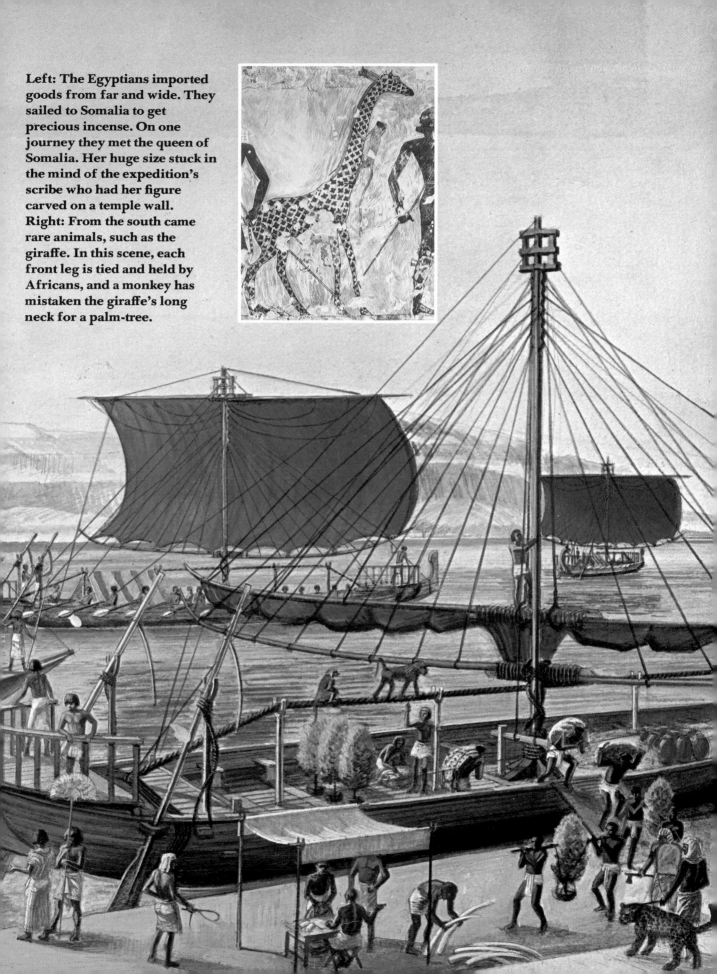

Left: The Egyptians imported goods from far and wide. They sailed to Somalia to get precious incense. On one journey they met the queen of Somalia. Her huge size stuck in the mind of the expedition's scribe who had her figure carved on a temple wall.

Right: From the south came rare animals, such as the giraffe. In this scene, each front leg is tied and held by Africans, and a monkey has mistaken the giraffe's long neck for a palm-tree.

Warfare

As a warleader the pharaoh had to protect Egypt's vulnerable frontiers facing Libya to the west and Palestine to the east. Part of a pharaoh's training was, therefore, to learn the martial arts such as archery. The pharaoh often carried a curved blade known as a scimitar, but the ordinary soldiers had a fairly basic weaponry: ox-hide shields, axes, clubs, wooden spears tipped with bronze, short swords and bows and arrows. Bow design was improved from a single shaft of wood to several layers of wood to give greater tautness and firing power.

The Egyptians used chariots with a light, curved frame made from wood with metal and leather coverings copied from the Hyksos invaders. Their main use was as a mobile firing platform for archers. Soldiers were grouped into divisions which had regimental emblems or standards under which they marched. Victorious commanders were awarded gold medals shaped like flies, and other jewellery. During

It was the pharaoh who led the Egyptian army in battle. Here a pharaoh, wearing his Blue Crown, charges into the thick of the enemy. His chariot is of light wood with leather and metal coverings over the body and round the wheels. Normally Egyptian chariots carried two soldiers, one to drive and one to fight, but pharaohs were often pictured alone to make them seem more heroic. The troops carry bronze-tipped spears and oxhide shields.

periods of peace, soldiers often had to do civilian work such as quarrying stone or working in the mines. Nubian warriors were also hired to serve in the Egyptian army and were highly regarded for their strength and fighting ability. The Shardana also fought for the Egyptians. These people were originally pirates and had distinctive horned helmets, long swords and round shields.

On campaigns abroad, scribes kept detailed diaries of the army's progress, and made sketches of any unusual plants or animals which they found on the way. On their return to Egypt these diaries were inscribed on the temple walls. There are records of the campaigns of King Tuthmosis III of Dynasty XVIII in the Middle East stretching over 20 years. One in particular tells of his bravery in crushing a rebellion of princes who had made their headquarters at a town in Palestine called Megiddo.

The travelling army carried light-weight equipment. We know that they took tents as their poles were imitated in the stone columns of one of Tuthmosis III's monuments. Folding stools covered with leopard skin were used by the army

commanders on campaigns. On the battlefield, trumpets were used to communicate with the troops and examples in gilded bronze and silver were found in Tutankhamun's tomb. According to some Egyptian writers there were many hardships in a soldier's life. Strict rules were enforced by beatings, and the soldiers were exhausted by long marches carrying provisions and army camp equipment, and lack of sleep from having to keep watch. In one account a wounded soldier travelled home to Egypt on the back of a donkey, only to have his clothes stolen on the way.

Above: Lightly armed Egyptian soldiers serve as an escort on a trade mission.
Left: An African army is utterly defeated by the pharaoh's troops. The Egyptians sometimes counted their dead enemies by piling up their cut-off hands.

Seth division

Ptah division

Egypt was rarely threatened by invasion from the sea, so sea battles were uncommon. However, Ramesses III of Dynasty XX fought a vital naval battle against invaders whom the Egyptians called the Sea Peoples. The enemy ships became trapped in one of the mouths of the Nile. Egyptian sailors used grappling hooks to pull the enemy boats close enough to destroy their masts and sails or capsize them. At the same time, archers and slingers aimed their shots carefully at the enemy look-outs and crews. From the shore the pharaoh and his soldiers fired a storm of arrows so that the water was filled with the bodies of the trapped invaders.

Fortresses in Ancient Egypt were positioned at strategic border areas facing possible land invasion routes from the west and east. Impressive mud-brick forts on the banks of the Nile in the far south controlled the movement of Nubians sailing on the river and protected the gold routes.

Ramesses II of Dynasty XIX has left us the story of his one important military campaign. He regarded it as a victory but it is clear that he barely escaped with his life. It was a battle fought against the Hittites from northern Turkey, and Syrian princes who threatened Egyptian interests in the Middle East. Ramesses led the Egyptian army towards the enemy stronghold at Kadesh on the river Orontes in Syria. Luckily he sent a detachment of assault troops by a different route. The army, consisting of both charioteers and infantry, was split into four divisions each of about 5,000 men, named after the

Above left: A chain of vast fortresses, built mainly of mud bricks, protected the gold shipments up and down the Nile from attack by marauding Nubians. Buhen fort, now lying under Lake Nasser, had ramparts, a steep moat, a drawbridge and a strong gate. The thick walls, 12 metres high, had bastions with loopholes for archers. Supplies were delivered by boat along the Nile.

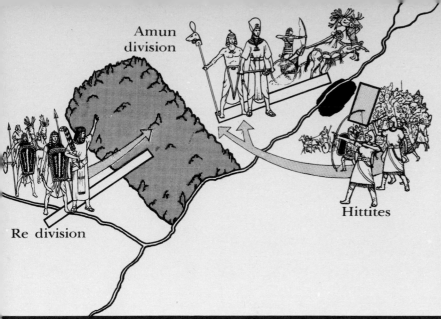

Amun division

Re division

Hittites

The Egyptians and Hittites fought at Kadesh. Ramesses II did not assemble all his 20,000 troops but marched ahead with his Amun division. Further back were the Re, Seth and Ptah divisions led by his sons. The pharaoh camped outside Kadesh, unaware of the enemy nearby. The Hittites attacked the Re division as it came out of the wood. They then turned on Ramesses' camp and almost killed the pharaoh before withdrawing.

Sea-fights were rare, but in one great battle, the lion-fronted ships of the Egyptians defeated the fleet of invading Sea Peoples. The sails were rolled up in case they got in the way of the fighters. Oarsmen pulled the enemy ships close so that archers, lancers and boarding parties could reach them.

gods Amun, Re, Seth and Ptah. Believing false information that the enemy had retreated 190 kilometres away, Ramesses and the division of Amun marched through a small forest to camp near Kadesh. The rest of the army was stretched out along the road for over 25 kilometres. To his horror, Ramesses learned from captured spies that the enemy were in fact right behind the town with 3,500 chariots and 9,000 infantry. Before Ramesses could takes steps to reorganize his army, the enemy attacked and the Egyptians panicked, deserting their leader who found himself surrounded by several thousand enemy chariots and soldiers. Despite his great bravery in battle, it was only the sudden arrival of the assault troops that saved the pharaoh's life. The enemy now lost the advantage, and their chariots were forced into the river. According to Ramesses' account, the Hittite leader almost drowned, and had to be held upside down by his men to shake the water out of him! The next day both sides decided on a cease-fire.

Everyday Life

Pictures in the tombs of Egyptian officials show scenes from the daily lives of people living thousands of years ago. The Egyptian nobleman enjoyed a comfortable family life. The garden of his villa would have a pool and shady fruit trees. The family enjoyed meals of beef, desert hares, gazelles, fruit such as pomegranates, figs and grapes, vegetables and bread. They might drink a vintage wine made from vines grown on the Delta.

For an evening party, people would dress elaborately and wear make-up. Over their own hair both men and women of rank wore fashionable wigs which were carefully combed, curled and braided. Children wore their hair in a single

Above: Ladies sit together at a party. One holds up a lotus to her friend. All wear dresses of finely pleated linen, and cones of perfumed animal fat on their heads. A girl serves a bowl of wine, and the table is loaded with fruit, meat, vegetables and bread.
Below: Musicians play the double-reeded flute, clap and sing. The song is written on the wall above them and praises the beauty of the world. Other women dance for the guests at this party. Garlands cover tall jars of wine or beer.

sidelock or a series of locks lying across their shaven scalps. A curious custom was the wearing of cones of perfumed fat over the wigs. During the warm evening the cone would melt and scented grease would spread over the wig.

Men wore long tunics with billowing sleeves while ladies' dresses were elaborately pleated in a variety of styles. Broad necklaces of brightly coloured beads were fashionable. On their feet the Egyptians wore sandals made of palm leaves, reeds or papyrus stalks. Their design was simple, merely soles with a narrow thong to secure the sandal to the foot.

Men and women made up their eyes most elaborately. The fashionable colours were green and grey. Both colours were made from minerals mixed with water to form a paste which was kept in tubes. The paste was applied to the skin around

Top: Cosmetic containers were often very elaborate. An alabaster jar is decorated with two Nile gods. They are shown knotting together the two plants, the papyrus and the lily, which symbolized Lower and Upper Egypt. This jar once held perfumed oil for the pharaoh Tutankhamun.
Above: Make-up was also kept in decorative spoons.
Right: An official's garden often contained a pool. Around it sycamores and palms would be planted to give shade.

the eye with a brush. Women painted their lips with red ochre which was also used as a rouge on the cheeks. Perfume was made from a variety of plants and seeds such as cinnamon and myrrh. Henna was used for staining the nails. Noblemen were usually clean-shaven or had only light beards.

On their arrival at a party, guests would be given mats or chairs with seats curved to take soft cushions. They would sit in groups, the married couples often sitting together on divans. Scantily clad serving girls gave the guests flowers and floral necklaces. They also handed round bowls of wine and such food as fruit, cakes and honeycombs. Musicians entertained the guests with harps, lutes, singing and rhythmic handclapping, and there were always beautiful dancers to watch. Sometimes the mixture of strong wine and rich food resulted in guests being ill which the Egyptians called 'sore hair'. After a party the aristocrat and his wife might go on to the roof of their villa and sit for a while in the refreshing night air. In their bedroom, they slept on low beds with cushioning, their feet towards a panelled board. They used headrests, usually of wood, softened by pillows for greater comfort.

Working-class Egyptians lived in wattle and daub huts or small mud-brick houses. They spent their days producing food or making goods and clothes for their masters, who were the estate owners and officials. Women had the task of pounding and crushing the grain for making bread. We can tell that Egyptian bread was quite coarse and gritty, because when mummies were examined, the teeth were found to be unusually worn down! Beer, drunk by all classes, was made from lightly baked loaves of barley bread. These were trodden into a watery mash by men standing in large pottery vats. The thick mixture was then poured through sieves into jars and stoppered.

Spinning factories worked by women kept the household in linen clothes made from the fibres of flax plants. Working men wore short linen kilts reinforced with leather netting across the seat. Serving girls wore long linen dresses, dyed in a plain colour such as green. Men would be responsible for laundering the clothes, and would beat them with sticks on rocks by the river.

At home, working people had few personal possessions. Oil lamps were a luxury so normally the family went to bed as soon as it got dark. Their staple diet would be bread with

vegetables like lentils, beans and onions. The men would catch fish or snare such small birds as quails in the fields. People also chewed papyrus stalks just as modern Egyptian children chew sugar cane.

There were many hazards in daily life in Ancient Egypt. Crocodiles lurked in the river, snakes and scorpions crawled into the houses from the desert, and various diseases were often picked up, especially from pools of stagnant water. Egyptian workers tried to prevent such dangers by magic and wore charms, shaped like the god Bes, on necklaces. Bes looked ugly and ferocious and the Egyptians believed that he protected the family against evil with his knife.

Egyptian families were usually large and it was always hoped that a new baby would be a boy. Magic spells were recited when children were born to invoke the help of the goddess Ta-weret, represented by a pregnant hippopotamus standing on its hind legs. Children were expected to help their parents with light work at home or in the fields as soon as they could. A son would take over his father's duties when the parent became too old for work. Many working people died during middle age and often the eldest son had to support two households, his own wife and children and also his younger brothers and sisters.

Above left: A house of plastered mud bricks. Wooden columns stand on stone bases and the ceiling is strengthened with palm logs. In the courtyard a woman makes bread while another produces thread for spinning. The granaries have hatches through which rations can be taken out. On the roof a woman weaves on the loom stretched out in front of her.
Below: Wooden models of servants at work were produced in large numbers and placed in tombs. The Egyptians thought they could come to life. One servant strains barley beer into a vat.
Below left: The hippopotamus-goddess watched over births.

Work

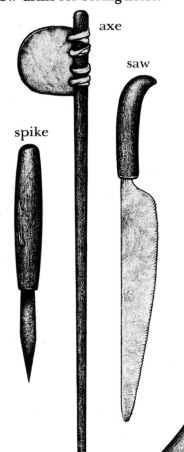

Above: An unkempt carpenter using an adze.
Below: The tools of the carpenter were simple. He used an adze to smoothe down surfaces. It consisted of a copper blade on a wooden shaft. Mallets were used to pound wood or stone, and bow-drills for boring holes.

axe

saw

spike

In western Thebes was a village which is today called Deir el Medina. Here the Egyptian workmen who built and decorated the royal tombs used to live. Theirs was a skilled job and the privilege of working in this secluded community was passed on from generation to generation. The village was some distance from the river Nile, so all food and drink, as well as clean linen clothes, had to be carried up to the village from the river bank. Let us look at a typical day when a foreman called Payson is getting ready to go to work.

He lived in a small mud-brick house off the main street of the village. At dawn he would go down into his cellar to collect his rations of barley bread and beer. The village was split into two groups, the 'left' and the 'right'. Payson was one of the foremen of these two groups. His 17 workers made up the 'left side of the gang'. One of Payson's first jobs was to go to the storehouse where the scribe weighed out the tools and equipment, such as wicks and oil for the lamps, needed to work in the deeper parts of the tomb, copper chisels for cutting the limestone, and plaster for smoothing over the walls. Payson would issue his workforce with their tools, and then he and his men followed a well-trodden path to the royal tomb in the Valley of the Kings. They stayed there for ten days at a time, sleeping in small huts. On arrival, a scribe would check to see that everyone was present. Payson would order from the tomb guardians the pigments for mixing paints and leather sacks for carrying the limestone flakes out of the tomb. Payson and his workmen realized their value to the king. There were occasions when the 'gang' did not receive their monthly rations and so they downed tools and staged a strike. The vizier himself had to negotiate with them so that work on the royal tomb would not be held up for too long.

Payson's men worked an eight hour day with a break for lunch. These were reasonable conditions when compared with life in the factories of nineteenth century Europe.

Right: The foreman collects copper tools for his men to cut out the pharaoh's tomb. A scribe records the weight of the tools so that they cannot be filed down before they are returned.

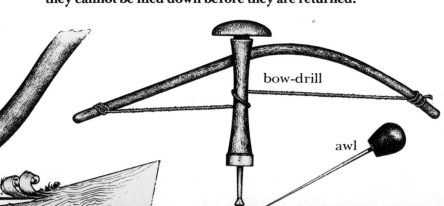

bow-drill

awl

adze

Below: The Egyptians imagined that life in the underworld could mean hard work. In a painting on his tomb wall, a nobleman called Sennedjem is shown reaping barley with a scythe, while his wife gathers the crop in a basket. The couple are also seen pulling up green stalks of flax to make linen. In a nearby scene, Sennedjem ploughs while his wife scatters seed. The underworld river ensures a good harvest and the trees at the bottom of the picture are weighed down with fruit.

Left: Paintings from Menna's tomb show what happened at harvest time. At the top, workers heap up the grain while scribes record the amount for Menna's tax records. Later, they will file their papyri in the chest shown above them. In the scene below, workers sift the grain with wooden trays. They wear pieces of linen to stop the chaff blowing into their hair. In the scene below this, large baskets are used to transport the crop for threshing. Two men are resting under a tree, where a waterskin hangs. Girls collect wisps of grain that have fallen to the ground and two of them are fighting over a handful.

As the whole of Egyptian society depended on crop-growing, most people worked in the fields alongside the Nile all their lives. Egyptian peasants were not slaves and many even owned some land of their own which, of course, they had to look after. However, they were also bound to rich lords who owned the majority of land along the river Nile. The peasants tended their masters' lands in return for a share of the produce, and their work was usually supervised by estate managers.

Agricultural work throughout the year depended on the rise and fall of the Nile. In winter, barley and a kind of wheat called emmer had to be sown on the rich Nile silt. The sower would walk along throwing the seed to the ground from a basket hanging around his neck. Two oxen followed behind pulling the plough which was guided by another worker. The heavy hoofs of the oxen helped to embed the seed firmly into the mud. The ploughshare itself was sometimes tipped with metal but if the ground was particularly hard, workers hoed it first to break it up. A flock of sheep would be driven behind the plough to tread the seed even further into the ground.

At harvest time, all the family would help to gather in the crops. Using scythes with flint blades, reapers cut the corn. Then the wheat was tied into sheaves, loaded on to donkeys, and taken off to be stacked in high piles. Much of this work was done to a rhythmic accompaniment made by men beating sticks together, and the chanting of songs. Women and children combed the fields after the men, cutting any ears of corn that had been missed, or picking up any grain that had fallen on to the ground. Women nursing young children were expected to help with light work in the fields with their children strapped to them in linen shawls. There were fixed rest times for the workers so that they could take a drink from their waterskins hanging in the branches of nearby trees, or have a nap in the shade.

The threshing would be done on a circle of hard ground or a round stone floor. One man would drive a pair of oxen round in a circle so that they crushed the grain with their hoofs. Other workers, with specially shaped trays, winnowed the corn to separate the grain from the husks by throwing it up into the air. The sifted corn could then be taken for storage to granaries which were carefully guarded against theft as the grain stocks were vital to the livelihood of the people. The granaries were either shaped like giant beehives, or were roughly square buildings with high walls and shuttered bins facing into a courtyard. From an upper level, an overseer could watch all the work being carried out in the yard below, and a foreman carefully recorded every sackful of grain that was taken away for use.

When the Nile was in flood, agricultural work could not take place. Each year, during August, September and October, the fieldworkers were sent off to labour on state-organized building projects, such as the pyramids. During these months, they received their pay in the form of rations from the granaries they had helped to fill during the summer.

An Egyptian estate was a hive of activity. In addition to the grain harvest there was the wine harvest. After the grapes had been plucked from the vine they were carried to troughs where men, clinging to the overhead trellis by short ropes to avoid slipping, trod the juice from them.

Elsewhere on the estate, men would be fattening up livestock. The force-feeding of cattle was a common practice. In tomb paintings we see oxen so overfed that their hoofs have become badly deformed under their weight. There are also wooden models of stables which show cattle so large that they could never have walked in through the door if the cattle had originally been the size of the models. Poultry, ducks and

Below: A worker operates the water-raising device called a shaduf. This is the oldest method of lifting water used in Egypt. A bucket on one end of a pole is dipped into the Nile or a canal. A clay or stone weight on the other end balances the pole. The bucket is then swung over and emptied into the fields or irrigation trenches.

Below: The best vineyards in Egypt were situated in the north which had a more Mediterranean climate. Clusters of ripe grapes were gathered from the vines. In the earliest pictures of wine-making, grapes were squeezed in a sack held between two men who twisted it tightly. Later on, grapes were taken to troughs where men trod them into juice. This was then poured into pottery jars, which were sealed with clay stoppers and stamped with the year of the pharaoh. Only the wealthy could afford wine to drink.

Below: At the opening of a
major canal, the vizier breaks
the clods of earth holding back
the Nile water, while officials,
under their district standards,
watch him. The leaders who
ruled Egypt before it was
united into one kingdom first
dug out canals from the Nile.
These took water to land close
to the desert making it possible
to grow crops there. The
pharaohs maintained the canal
network. The canals were
regularly cleared of silt, and
the mud forming the banks had
to be kept firm. This sort of
work was done by ordinary
Egyptians called up by the state
during the periods when they
were not needed in the fields.

long-necked cranes were force-fed by having pellets of food
pushed down their beaks.

There was a plentiful supply of such fish as perch in the
Nile. Men with dragnets made large catches and sometimes a
boatman was able to pull up a giant catfish by its whiskers! Fish
were cut open and left to dry. Trapping birds and ducks was
another activity and it was not difficult. Framed nets were set
around a pool in the papyrus thickets. One man hid close by
and others were concealed further away holding a rope
attached to the nets. When enough birds had landed on the
pool the look-out leapt up and signalled with a white scarf.
The men pulled the rope and the nets collapsed over the pool.

The canal system, that fed the fields with water after the
annual flood had receded, was continually being repaired and
new canals were dug. Water was raised up from the Nile to
canals on the higher level by means of a *shaduf*, which is still
commonly used in Egypt today. The Greeks and Romans
introduced the 'Archimedes' screw', which was a hollow
cylinder with a corkscrew-like device inside. When the screw
was turned, it lifted up the river water to the level of the bank.
Finally, there was the *sakia*, a water-wheel operated by oxen.

Arts and Crafts

Although we do not know their names, the craftsmen of Ancient Egypt have provided us with a lot of information about life in those days. Commissioned by the king, temple priests or officials, these skilled workmen laboured to please the pharaoh or gods, or to make a nobleman's afterlife in the tomb easier. Skills were passed on from fathers to their sons, who became their apprentices.

Sculptors used stone from different parts of Egypt for their work. Quarries around Memphis provided high-quality limestone for the pyramids, while from the south came sandstone from which most of the great Theban temples were made. At Aswan there were the granite quarries. The Egyptians worked these extensively, but used only the simplest of tools.

A statue was begun by the front and side views of the design being outlined in paint on a cube of stone. The sculptors then began chiselling the stone from these two directions—the backs of statues were often left flat. When the figure was recognizable the contours were expertly shaped by the master-sculptor. The statue was then ready to be painted. Normally, on statues of women the skin was painted a pale yellowy colour, while men were coloured a reddish brown. A typical style of statue shows an official standing with his left foot forward and his arms by his sides with hands gripping stylised sceptres of which only the handles are shown. He wears a short kilt and broad necklace. The face has a slight smile and is not a true but an idealized portrait. The sculptor sometimes showed an official with rolls of fat on his chest and

Above: A limestone statue from the Old Kingdom showing an official and his wife. Their faces are not meant to be realistic portraits but idealized versions of how they wanted to look. This Egyptian couple would have believed that their spirits would recognize their names carved on the base of the statue, and could enter into the figures and bring them to life.
Below: A huge statue of a high priest in the Temple of Karnak.

Above: Egyptian artists followed rules set down in very early times, which to us look rather strange. Only one eye was depicted and was drawn as if from the front (from the side, it could not be seen clearly). The head, chest and legs were drawn in profile, but the shoulders were always drawn from the front.

stomach. This was a sign of prosperity. Occasionally the Egyptians carved realistic portraits showing perhaps an old man with lines and furrows on his face.

Before decorating a rock tomb, at Thebes for example, men and boys smoothed down the walls and covered the rock with limestone plaster. Draughtsmen had a special selection of scenes designed for tombs. They divided the tomb wall up into squares, and then transferred on to it an enlarged version of the same picture drawn as a small, similarly squared, rough sketch. By their 'canon (rule) of proportions', parts of the human body fitted into a fixed number of squares.

When an official's tomb had been cut out of the rock, craftsmen spent years decorating its walls and ceiling. Rough surfaces were coated with limestone plaster. A scene drawn in miniature on a flake of stone was then transferred on to the squared-up wall. This allowed large areas to be covered easily. The squares were also useful for drawing people. Artists had a set number of squares for each portion of the body. There were three squares for the head, for example. This system was called the 'canon of proportions'.

**Right: Colourful glass was
used to make jewellery and
scent bottles. It was shaped in
moulds, or made into strips of
molten glass which were
twisted round wire. The wire
was removed when the glass
had cooled.
Right centre: This collar,
decorated with gold hawk
heads, once belonged to a
queen. The rows of beads are
made of cornelian and
turquoise, and the hawks' eyes
are obsidian. Cheaper green
manufactured beads were also
used, but most of these have
decayed.
Below right: Tutankhamun
was buried with his fan. It once
bore 30 ostrich feathers but
over the centuries insects have
eaten them. Gold sheets cover a
wooden core. The goldsmith
has beaten out a scene of the
pharaoh's ostrich hunt.**

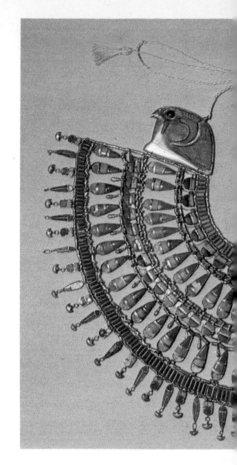

Objects and paintings found in tombs show us the exquisite craftsmanship of the Egyptians in jewellery and metalwork. The jeweller's beads were made from semi-precious stones found in the deserts and Sinai peninsula. They included violet amethyst, red carnelian, green felspar and blue turquoise. One highly prized stone, dark-blue lapis lazuli, was obtained from Middle Eastern merchants. Colour was the most important aspect of Egyptian jewellery so that the materials did not necessarily have to be valuable, but could be imitated by powdered and coloured quartz paste, often called *faience*. The Egyptians also used coloured glass which they poured into moulds or drew into thin strips. These cheaper materials would not only be used for the jewellery of ordinary Egyptians but even for royalty. Some *faience* and glass, which looks like lapis lazuli, occur in Tutankhamun's splendid gold mask.

Holes were made in beads by pressing down on a thin, metal-tipped drill rotated by a bow pushed backwards and forwards as seen on page 20. Egypt had plenty of gold, from deep mines in the sand, and quartz rocks in its deserts. An Egyptian jeweller was called a 'gold man'. He was able to hammer the gold into shape, as in the hollow armbands awarded by the pharaoh for state service, or the thin sheets which were used to cover wooden furniture and coffins. He

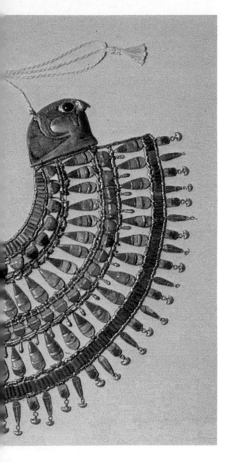

A bronze statuette of Bastet, the cat-goddess, was first made of wax, coated with clay and baked. The melted wax escaped through a hole. Molten bronze was then poured into the clay shell and left to harden. The clay was removed and the remaining bronze sculpture was polished.

could also cast it, draw it into wire, or attach minute beads of it to a plain metal surface with solder. Workmen were also able to engrave or emboss the gold. Iron was not widely used by metal workers except for special objects such as the blade of one of Tutankhamun's daggers. The Egyptians had to import silver and during times of scarcity it became more valuable than gold. One pharaoh had his entire coffin made of silver.

Many statues of pharaohs and gods were made from copper and its alloy, bronze. These were often covered with gold leaf to make them appear more precious. Copper mines produced an unlimited supply of the metal for the palace and temple workshops. Craftsmen melted the copper and bronze by heating it over a furnace. To get the high temperature required, air was blasted into the fire. This was first done by blowing the air through long tubes. A common method of making a bronze statuette was by the 'lost wax' technique. A figure of, for example, the cat-goddess or bull-god was first made out of beeswax. It was then coated with clay and heated so that the wax melted and poured away through specially cut small holes. Liquid bronze was then poured into the baked clay mould and left to set. After the mould was broken away, the solid bronze statuette was ready for its final chiselling and polishing. To economize on bronze this method could be slightly changed to produce a hollow statuette.

Religion

The Egyptians worshipped many gods and goddesses of ancient origin, and every important town and district was the cult centre for a local god. This god could appear in the world perhaps in human form, like Min the fertility-god, or perhaps as an animal, such as Apis the bull-god, or Sobek the crocodile-god. Priests in the temples kept possibly one or even thousands of the animal sacred to their god. When these animals died they were mummified and buried near the sanctuary of the god or goddess to whom they were sacred.

The Egyptians tried to explain how they thought the world was created. For example, at Heliopolis, the ancient centre of sun-worship, the priests believed that originally there was

Left: Osiris was the ruler of the underworld. It was in his power to give any Egyptian eternal life. His 'Atef' crown is made of two plumes, a tall cone and the horns of his sacred animal, the ram. Like the pharaohs, he holds a crook and flail.
Right: The goddess Isis, wife of Osiris, nurses her son Horus, who grew up to avenge his father's murder.

Thoth

Horus

Maat

Amun-Re

Many districts in Egypt worshipped sacred animals. Crocodiles, for example, were worshipped in the south and the Fayyum, but in other areas they could be killed on sight. The cat was sacred to the goddess Bastet, whose chief temple was in the Delta. Here one has been mummified and carefully wrapped. A bronze headpiece would be fixed on and the mummy put into a cat-shaped coffin.

nothing except a watery mass called Nun. Out of it rose the sun-god, Re-Atum, also known by the name Khepri, the scarab-beetle. Re-Atum spat out the next pair of beings, who were the god Shu, or air, and the goddess Tefnut, or moisture. These two mated to produce the earth-god Geb and the sky-goddess Nut. At Memphis, the capital, there was a very different kind of belief about the creation whereby the god Ptah merely thought of the world and the other gods, and then magically spoke them into existence.

All kinds of myths and stories grew up about the gods and their family rivalries. In the distant past, the Egyptians believed that their country was ruled by the god Osiris and enjoyed a 'Golden Age' when there was prosperity for everyone. Seth, the brother of Osiris, was jealous and plotted to kill Osiris and seize the throne. At a banquet, Seth promised a valuable chest to anyone who could fit into it exactly. When Osiris got inside, the lid was closed, the chest was tied up and thrown into the Nile. Isis, the wife of Osiris, managed to rescue his body. She kept it in the Delta marshes but while she was absent Seth, out on a hunting trip, came across it. He chopped the body into pieces and scattered them up and down Egypt. Isis collected nearly all the parts and Anubis the jackal-god helped her to wrap them in linen bandages, so forming the first mummy. Because Isis was 'great in magic' she brought Osiris sufficiently to life to make her pregnant. Osiris then left this world to become ruler of the Kingdom of the Dead. Isis gave birth to a son, Horus. At last, Horus became old enough to avenge his father's murder and regain the throne. A vicious struggle lasted for years between Horus and Seth but, at last, Horus took his claim to the court of the gods where he won his inheritance of the kingship of Egypt.

Below: Egyptian gods. Thoth, the ibis-headed god of knowledge, taught man hieroglyphs. Hawk-headed Horus was a sky-god and the son of Isis and Osiris. Maat, the sun-god's daughter, represented correct behaviour. Amun-Re of Thebes was king of the gods. Anubis, the jackal-god, ruled over embalmers and cemeteries. Khnum, the ram-god, made man on a potter's wheel. Re-Horakhti was the rising sun. Ptah of Memphis was an important creator-god and patron of craftsmen.

Anubis

Khnum

Re-Horakhti

Ptah

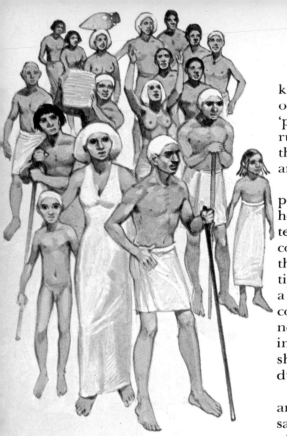

The priests of Ancient Egypt who staffed the temples were known as 'servants of the god'. At the top was the high priest often called the 'first prophet'. Less powerful priests known as 'pure ones' were responsible for keeping the daily routine running smoothly. It was the custom for priests to shave off their body hair and not eat certain foods. Priestesses were arranged in their own hierarchy.

The temple itself was the 'house of the god', and ordinary people were not allowed to enter it. A thick mud wall enclosed houses for the priests and storerooms. The entrance to the temple was through a massive gateway called a *pylon* which consisted of two towers on each side of the door. Just before the pylon there were often two obelisks, sometimes with their tips sheathed with electrum, which was a mixture of gold with a little silver. Inside the temple was a *hypostyle hall,* a court containing a forest of columns to support the roof. There was not much light as the windows consisted of tiny grills high up in the walls. Beyond this was the sanctuary where the god's shrine rested in utter darkness, lit only by the priests' lamps during rituals.

Daily rituals in the temple provided the god with all his food and needs. In the morning the high priest entered the sanctuary and opened the shrine containing the golden image of the god. The god was awakened, dressed in fresh linen and given breakfast. At night the shrine was bolted while the god slept.

On the western bank of the Nile at Thebes, pharaohs built funerary temples or 'mansions of millions of years' as they were called. The walls of these temples often showed notable events of the ruler's reign. For example, Queen Hatshepsut's terraced temple at Deir el Bahari commemorated the transport of her two granite obelisks, each weighing at least 500 tonnes, from Aswan up to Thebes.

There were, of course, rivalries between the temples of different religious cults. For over 2,000 years, Amun-Re the sun-god was in favour. Then, a new pharaoh, Akhenaten, forced his own brand of sun worship on the people and closed all the temples to the other gods. However when Akhenaten died his successor Tutankhamun re-opened the temples and Amun-Re reigned supreme once more.

Above: Ordinary people rarely got inside a temple. But on festival days they lined the processional way to watch the priests carry the god's shrine. Below: A typical lay-out of a temple. The first court behind the pylon was used for public offerings, but the halls, chapels and sanctuary were restricted to priests.

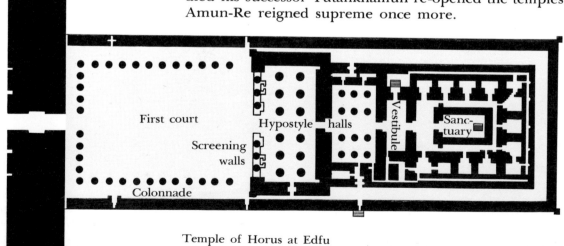

First court

Screening walls

Colonnade

Hypostyle halls

Vestibule

Sanc-tuary

Temple of Horus at Edfu

Pylon

In the temple, the high priest wakes up the statue of the god Amun-Re. As he removes the linen shawl another priest is about to put a pellet of incense in the burner.

The Ancient Egyptians were very practical people and took steps to ensure that their lives never came to an end. The tomb was to be the 'house of eternity'. Also, they tried to preserve the body artificially by a process that we call 'mummification'.

When a person of rank died, his corpse was taken to the 'house of purification'. Embalmers removed the soft organs such as the brain, intestine, lungs and stomach, which could cause the flesh to putrefy. The heart was deliberately left inside the body. Then the embalmers extracted all the water from the body by covering it with solid natron (a sodium carbonate compound) which dried it out in 40 days. The internal organs were similarly dried out and put into four containers later to be buried with the body. The corpse was rubbed with perfumed ointments and sometimes artificial eyes were inserted to give the face a more life-like appearance. The body was wrapped in linen bandages in which magical charms or 'amulets' were placed, often made of gold. By the time the priests had finished reciting the correct rituals over the body, 70 days had passed since the person's death. The coffin, in the shape of a mummified body, portrayed the idealized face of the dead person and was decorated with such gods and goddesses as the jackal Anubis and the sky-goddess Nut.

The coffin would then be placed on a sledge and dragged to the tomb, accompanied by women who tore their clothes, threw dust over their hair and wailed. Servants carried boxes of clothes and jewellery. At the tombside the coffin was held upright for a vital ritual known as 'opening the mouth'. It gave the dead person power to eat, speak, drink and move about in the tomb. The body and grave-goods were finally sealed in the tomb by rubble.

Above: The body of the pharaoh Tutankhamun is embalmed. The internal organs have been dried out and put into an alabaster chest. The tops of each of its four compartments are carved with the head of the pharaoh. Meanwhile, priests chant spells and burn incense.
Left: The priestess Anhai, led by Horus, watches her heart weighed against the goddess of truth. If her heart does not balance, it will be chewed up by the crocodile-headed monster Ammut.
Right: The mummy case of a Theban priest.

Two parts of the soul, the Ka and the Ba, remained in the tomb. A third part called the Akh went below the burial chamber into the Kingdom of Osiris, called Duat. There the dead person had to pass an examination in the 'hall of the two truths' to prove that he was good enough to live in Osiris' realm. The dead person's heart was put on a pair of scales and weighed against the goddess of truth. The dead man had to deny that he had committed crimes such as blasphemy, stealing milk from babies, damaging temple property and murder. If he was found guilty, then Ammut the devourer, a hybrid creature made up from a crocodile, lion and hippopotamus, would chew up the heart and annihilate him. If his heart balanced evenly he was not guilty, and Thoth, god of wisdom, recorded the verdict. In Duat the Egyptians thought there was a paradise rather like Egypt itself. They called it 'Re's field of reeds' where there was always enough food, fresh water, cool breezes, and sycamore trees to rest under for all eternity.

Buildings

The Egyptians were the first to use stone to build large monuments. Imhotep, the architect of King Zoser of Dynasty III, designed and organized the building of the earliest pyramid in stone at Saqqara, overlooking the capital city of Memphis. This step pyramid, which rose in six steps to a height of 60 metres, symbolized a gigantic stairway into the sky by which the pharaoh could ascend to his father, the Sun-god. It was built of desert stone with its outer casing made of high-quality limestone.

The pharaohs of Dynasty IV adapted Imhotep's plan into pyramids with sloping sides. In the desert at Giza there still are splendid examples of such pyramids belonging to Cheops, Chephren and Mycerinus. The Great Pyramid of Cheops consists of several million blocks of stone, some weighing about 15 tonnes. In this pyramid the burial chamber is at the core of the superstructure. A series of five gaps were built above this chamber preventing the roof collapsing onto the pharaoh's sarcophagus.

Pyramid building was a very costly operation and a great drain on the country's resources. In later dynasties the pharaohs were buried at Thebes, in the Valley of the Kings,

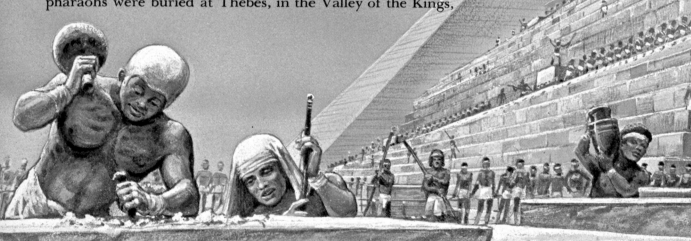

where their tombs were simply cut into the hillside. A long passageway was usually built which led into a deep pit or well. The purpose of this was to trap any rainwater seeping into the tomb, and to hinder robbers. However, thieves scaled these pits using rope ladders, and continued through another passageway hidden behind a decorated wall into the burial chamber, or 'hall of gold', which contained the granite sarcophagus of the pharaoh. The walls of the burial chamber and corridors were smoothed with limestone plaster and covered with religious scenes. High-ranking officials were also buried in the Valley of the Kings. The famous young king Tutankhamun was not buried in a typical royal tomb. His tomb was small and was originally intended for his vizier.

Left: The tomb of Ramesses VI cut out of the rock in the Valley of the Kings. Colourful scenes of gods of the underworld decorate the walls. The sarcophagus of the pharaoh has been smashed and robbed. Right: A plan of the Great Pyramid of Cheops at Giza. Originally it was 146 metres high and covered an area at its base of over 5 hectares. Unlike other pyramids, the burial chamber is above ground level.

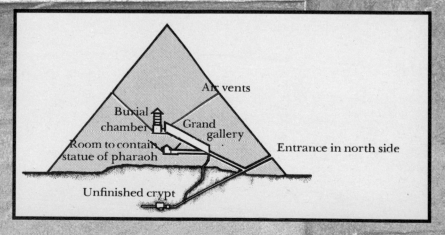

Air vents

Burial chamber

Grand gallery

Entrance in north side

Room to contain statue of pharaoh

Unfinished crypt

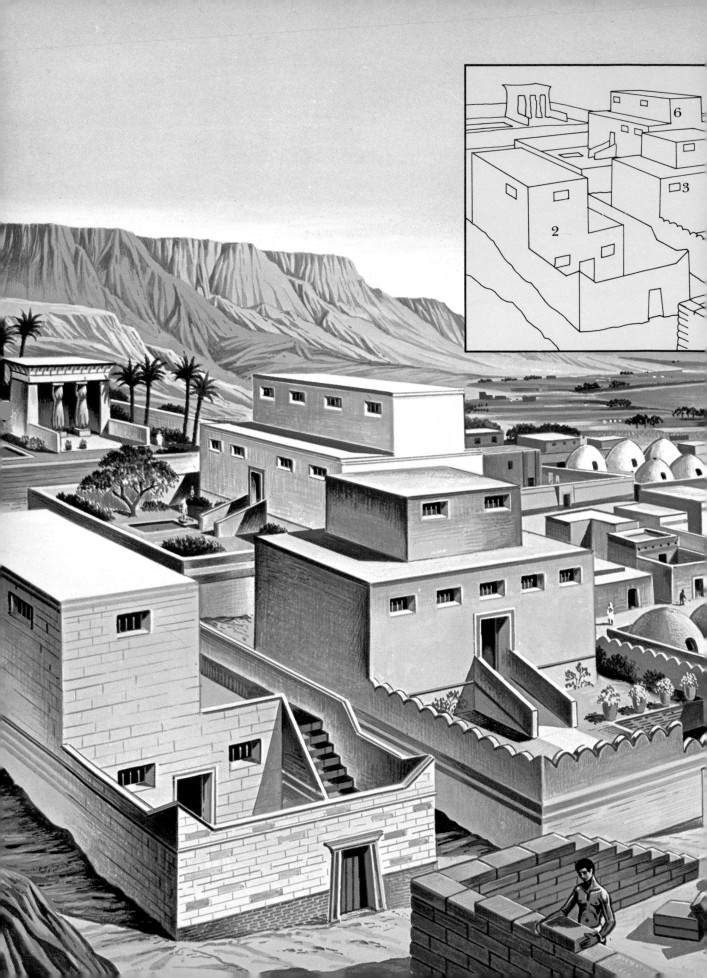

Left: An Egyptian village.
1 Making bricks of Nile mud using wooden frames. Bricks were left in the sun to dry.
2 Mud-brick houses were cool in summer, warm in winter.
3 Grill windows were cut high in the plastered walls to stop direct sunshine. 4 Domes stored barley and wheat. Overseers carefully noted sackfuls taken out. 5 Roof-top rooms, open on one side, caught cool breezes. 6 An official's pavilion. He often inspected cattle here. 7 Poorer Egyptians put up huts of mud and bundles of reeds.

Above: An excavation in progress at Thebes. From the sand and rubble, the archaeologist's spade has unearthed the foundations of temples and towns.

Most of the everyday buildings of early Egypt were made out of mud bricks, from the villas of the aristocrats to the craftsmen's workshops and the houses of ordinary people. Bundles of reeds tied together were used for the walls and ceilings of the huts of the poorer people.

Making mud bricks was quite simple. Men would cut up the mud on the banks of the Nile and carry it to the town. Water from a nearby pool was then mixed with the mud to keep it pliable. Sometimes chopped straw was added to bind the mud together. Men with moulds then formed the bricks and left them in rows in the sun to dry. This was one of the jobs in which prisoners-of-war helped out the Egyptian workers. After finishing a building, the outside walls were often covered with white plaster, making them gleam in the sunlight. Inside, the walls could be decorated with reed hangings or painted with scenes such as ducks in flight.

There was, as a rule, no organized town-planning. Several main streets usually divided the town. The nobles chose the best sites for their villas and faced them towards the north in order to catch any cool breezes.

Walls surrounded the villas of high-ranking Egyptians and enclosed a pool and a garden with trees. Important officials also had dome-shaped granaries and stables for cattle, as well as living quarters for servants. The villa itself had only small windows, high up in the walls to keep out the hot glare of the sun. There was a central reception room, perhaps with wooden pillars supporting a ceiling of palm logs. Doorways off this room led to the kitchen, bedrooms, and a bathroom, which was fitted with a lavatory and shower facilities. Stairs led up to the roof to a small shaded loggia.

Simpler houses for the poorer people sometimes had courtyards for their ducks and sheep, with cellars and jars sunk into the ground for storing food or valuables. The common way to dispose of all kinds of waste was to pile it haphazardly in heaps or on town dumps.

Education
and Learning

In Egyptian society everything that had to be recorded, such as state policies, the daily organization of the work-force, and accounting, was in the hands of an educated group of people called scribes.

A boy wishing to become a scribe had a rigorous education lasting about six years at a school attached to an estate, temple or palace. Lessons were enforced by the cane because it was said that a pupil's ear was 'on his back'. Truancy was tempting, especially when a boy could see his friends playing games. He had to be frequently reminded that one day, by being a scribe, he would be better off than a soldier, fieldworker or craftsman. Pupils had to copy out exercises consisting, for example, of model letters, lists of the names of foreign towns and countries, or excerpts from Egyptian stories. Many 'school books' on flakes of limestone or papyri have survived.

Various scripts were used in early Egypt and pupils had to be able to write them all. Hieroglyphs are picture signs and there were over 700 to be learned. Some hieroglyphs stand for

Below: In a temple school, the tutor teaches boys to use brushes to make hieroglyphs in their 'exercise-books'.

Left: Hieroglyphs were always used for formal and religious writing. In this form of script, pictures were used to spell out words. Egyptian scribes drew over 700 separate symbols including birds, animals, a man dancing, a boy sucking his finger, boats, weapons, plants, home-utensils and buildings. The hieroglyphs shown here are read from top to bottom, but they could also be written horizontally. Horizontal hieroglyphs can be read from left to right or right to left—the beaks of the birds point to the start.
Below left: A papyrus written in Hieratic script. Hieratic was written from right to left.
Below: Common hieroglyphs often seen on Egyptian monuments.

single sounds and are used to spell out words phonetically, e.g. the hieroglyph for 'M' is a picture of an owl. Other hieroglyphs represent whole words by a single picture, e.g. a boat or a bull.

The everyday writing material was papyrus. Black ink was made from soot, and red ink, which was used mostly for headings, was made from ochre. A scribe sat cross-legged on the ground, stretching his kilt taut across his knees to act as a desk, and wrote on the papyrus from right to left with a reed brush. He found he could write more quickly if the picture signs were abbreviated to just a few strokes. This style of script is called 'Hieratic'. In the seventh century B.C., an even more rapid and cursive script, called 'Demotic', came into use for business and legal documents.

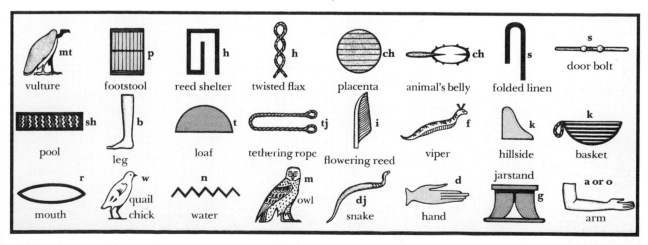

mt vulture	**p** footstool	**h** reed shelter
h twisted flax	**ch** placenta	**ch** animal's belly
s folded linen	**s** door bolt	
sh pool	**b** leg	**t** loaf
tj tethering rope	**i** flowering reed	**f** viper
k hillside	**k** basket	
r mouth	**w** quail chick	**n** water
m owl	**dj** snake	**d** hand
g jarstand	**a or o** arm	

41

Above: Egyptians called the stars 'imperishable ones'. This ceiling shows the northern constellations of the sky as gods and animals. The bull, with the man behind it, forms the Great Bear, while the hawk-god is the Swan. However, the star groups cannot all be identified with constellations we see today.

The scribes had access to all the available knowledge of mathematics, astronomy and medicine, stored on papyrus rolls in a reference library known as the 'House of Life'. The scribes' libraries also contained plans for the royal tombs detailing the various rooms and corridors, and maps giving routes through the desert to the gold mines. Science in Ancient Egypt was of a practical kind. Arithmetic centred around problems like the calculation of areas and volumes for building projects or measuring fields, or keeping accounts of the distribution of grain rations to workmen. The standard unit of measurement was the cubit—the distance from elbow to finger tips. It was calculated at about 50 centimetres for the Royal Cubit and about 43 centimetres for the short cubit. Ready-reckoners on papyri have been found for helping the scribe in his calculations. Other papyri give set solutions to problems. To multiply one number by another the scribes had quite a long and complicated method involving doubling and addition. For example to multiply 20 by five they doubled 20 and its results until they had as near five units as possible:

$$1 \times 20 = 20$$
$$2 \times 20 = 40$$
$$4 \times 20 = 80$$
$$8 \times 20 = 160$$

I	=	1
∩	=	10
℮	=	100
↓	=	1,000
∫	=	10,000
𝕝	=	100,000
𝕪	=	1,000,000

14	=	∩ IIII
76	=	∩∩∩∩ ∩∩∩ IIIIII
302	=	℮℮℮II

Numbers in Egypt were written as multiples of ten or more using the symbols of a coil, lotus, finger and tadpole. The god of infinity represented 'millions'. Scribes grouped these signs to make any number needed.

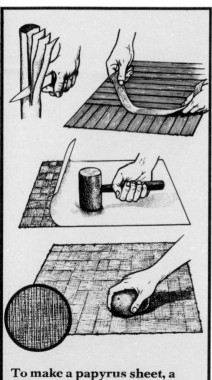

To make a papyrus sheet, a papyrus stalk was peeled and thinly sliced. Two crossed layers were hammered under a linen covering and smoothed by a stone.

They then added the results opposite the numbers adding up to five, i.e. 1+4. Therefore 20+80=100. Their method of division seems just as cumbersome to our eyes.

The ordinary Egyptian simply based his farming calendar around the annual flood of the Nile. However, there was also a more formal 'state' calendar worked out by the scribes which was extremely accurate. The year was divided up into twelve months of 30 days each. At the end of the year five extra days (regarded as birthdays for the gods) were added to bring the total to 365. The day itself was broken up into 24 hours—12 for day and 12 for night—varying in length according to the season. By dividing the rising of the stars across the sky into 36 constellations the Egyptians worked out a star-clock, enabling scribes and priests to calculate the hour of the night. The constellations were depicted as human or animal figures such as the crocodile, lion or hippopotamus, but most of the stars shown cannot be identified today.

Egyptian doctors were also priests of the ferocious lion-goddess Sekhmet. They learned anatomy by studying the carcasses of sacrificed animals and the organs removed from humans during mummification. Magical spells had to be recited over the sick person (especially in the case of snake or scorpion bites), and drugs made from animals and plant products, including bats, bees, frogs, mice and vultures, were given. Treatises were written describing symptoms and suggesting treatments for ailments such as rheumatism, toothache, eye diseases (treated by specialist doctors), bone fractures and upset stomachs. Some very interesting papyri survive which contain studies on the heart and on childbirth.

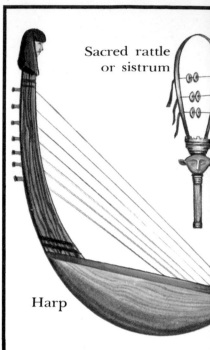

Sacred rattle or sistrum

Harp

Above: A scribe's cartoon, drawn on papyrus. Egyptians loved to show animals acting like people. Here, a lion and an antelope sit opposite each other, playing the popular board game 'senet'. The joke is that the two animals are enemies in the wild.

Sports and Pastimes

Egyptians of rank used to enjoy hunting desert animals. Tomb paintings show scenes in which antelopes, wild oxen, foxes and deer are fleeing to avoid the hunter's arrows or a pack of hounds. Tutankhamun seems to have been fond of hunting ostriches from his chariot, and Ramesses III liked spearing wild bulls in the marshes. Another king was so proud of the 102 lions that he killed in a period of ten years that he issued a news bulletin to commemorate it. A king's education included training in such sports as archery or hunting as he needed to show his people that his bravery and skill were superhuman. One king boasted of how he was able to shoot arrows from a moving chariot completely through copper targets over 11 metres away.

Egyptian nobles liked to take their families out for a day's sport when they would enjoy spearing fish or stunning ducks in the marshes with 'throwsticks'. Hunting hippopotami was more dangerous so a nobleman would watch while his servants in papyrus canoes lassoed the animals and speared them.

Wrestling appears to have been a popular recreation and there were a large number of set holds and manoeuvres for throwing an opponent. Boys and girls, too, enjoyed catching balls or playing energetic games, some of them similar to leapfrog. They also practised acrobatics such as turning

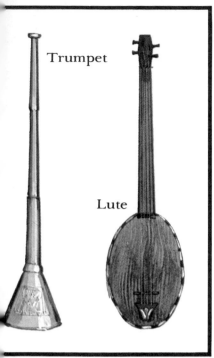

Trumpet

Lute

somersaults. Indoor games included *senet* in which two people moved counters around a rectangular board divided up into squares. It is thought that the first counter to move down the centre was the winner. Another game was a race to the middle of a board which was in the shape of a coiled snake. For amusement children also had such toys as tiny model leopards whose jaws could be opened and shut by pulling a string, small wooden horses on wheels, or dolls made of mud or carved from a flat piece of wood.

At parties, entertainment was provided by an orchestra, usually of women. They played harps of varying sizes, lyres and double-reed flutes, and clapped their hands and sang. The strong percussion section of the orchestra included drums, clappers, tambourines and instruments called *crotals* In rhythm to this music, girls often dressed only in girdles, danced. Music was a profession which included blind people who were trained to play the harp and sing.

Below: The royal scribe, Userhat, quiver on his back, chases desert animals. He steers his chariot by the reins tied round his waist. In real life he would have a driver. The horses stretch out in a gallop while Userhat's arrows strike antelopes, hares and hyenas.

Discovering Ancient Egypt

In 1798 the French general Napoleon led his army into Egypt. Scientists and antiquarians went with him and recorded everything they saw, including details of rocks and minerals, flowers, animals, scenes of contemporary life and ancient ruins. The publication of their notes and drawings in the *Déscription de l'Égypte* forms the first 'modern' study of Egypt.

One of the most famous experts in Egyptian archaeology was the Englishman Sir W. Flinders Petrie. His imagination was fired when he first went to Egypt to survey the pyramids at Giza. His painstaking methods of digging sites involving the strict supervision of workmen, the recording of every detail, and his system of dating by pottery shapes, set new standards in Egyptian archaeology.

In 1922 the British archaeologist Howard Carter's intuition that a small unexcavated area of the Valley of the Kings might be worth investigating resulted in the discovery of the glittering gold of the Tomb of Tutankhamun. The spectacular objects buried with the young pharaoh still excite wonder today.

Below: The 30-metre-high rock temple of Ramesses II at Abu Simbel. Originally carved in the Nile's bank, engineers rebuilt it at a higher level to prevent its disappearance under a new lake.

Above: Born in France in 1790, Jean-François Champollion dedicated his life to Ancient Egypt. In 1822, he managed to crack the code of hieroglyphs which had fallen out of use over 1,500 years before. Below: A soldier in Napoleon's army found this stone at Rosetta in the Delta. The same message is written on it in two languages. The top scripts are Egyptian written in hieroglyphs and Demotic. The bottom script is Greek. This stone was crucial in helping Champollion to discover how to read the hieroglyphs.

Above: During the 19th century many large statues were taken from Egypt. Belzoni, a circus strong man, shipped the seven-and-a-half-tonne granite head of Ramesses II to the British Museum. Below: Inside the tiny tomb of Tutankhamun.

In more recent times, the damming of the Nile to control its annual flood has posed a threat to many ancient sites. The temples of Abu Simbel were actually moved from their original site to save them from being flooded. Many sites that could not be saved had to be studied and recorded and, as a result, archaeologists from many countries came together to work against the clock. Finally, in Egypt today, teams of archaeologists from Europe and America are working alongside their Egyptian colleagues to discover the tombs and buildings which are still believed to be lying below the sand.

Glossary

AMULETS: Magical charms often connected with a particular god or goddess. They could be worn as jewellery for protection in daily life or included in the mummy wrappings to safeguard the corpse.

BA: The soul in the form of a bird's body with a human head. The Egyptians believed that it was able to flit around the burial chamber and journey outside the tomb.

BOOK OF THE DEAD: The modern name given to the Egyptian 'Book of Coming Out by Day'. It was a collection of spells and pictures on a papyrus roll and was buried near or on the dead person to help him on his journey through the underworld.

DEMOTIC: An Egyptian script which came into vogue in the seventh century B.C. and was used extensively on papyri for writing letters, and business and legal documents.

EMBALMER: Someone who preserves corpses from decay. In early Egyptian times this was done by 'mummification'.

HIERATIC: A script in which the hieroglyphs have been simplified into less detailed pen strokes. This was the usual kind of writing for accounts, business and administration, and story-books.

HIEROGLYPHS: The earliest Egyptian form of writing. It used pictures to indicate the sounds that made up a word. It was always used as the formal script for stone monuments of a religious or commemorative nature, such as are found in temples or tombs.

HYPOSTYLE HALL: The name given to a temple court which contains rows of columns supporting a roof.

KA: The personality and spirit of a person, identical in form to the human body, and brought into existence at the same time as a person is conceived. After death it continues a life in the tomb centred around the mummy or statues of the dead person.

MUMMIFICATION: The artificial preservation of a corpse by dehydrating it and removing the internal organs likely to decay.

PAPYRUS: A reed which grew along the banks of the Nile and was used to make writing materials, canoes, rope and sandals. It no longer grows naturally in Egypt.

PHARAOH: The word comes originally from the Ancient Egyptian 'per-ao' which means 'great house' and was used to describe the king's palace. It came to be used as a respectful term for the king himself.

PYLON: The gateway to a temple. It consisted of two massive towers flanking the entrance, adorned with reliefs of the pharaoh and gods. Originally, tall flagpoles were supported against them.

PYRAMIDS: Tombs for the pharaohs, dating mainly from the Old Kingdom when the Great Pyramid at Giza was built. The first pyramid was a series of six stages forming steps. Later, the steps were filled in to become true pyramids with sloping sides.

ROSETTA STONE: A basalt slab, now in the British Museum, inscribed in three different scripts—Hieroglyphs, Demotic and Greek. It gave Champollion the key to deciphering Ancient Egyptian writing.

SARCOPHAGUS: A rectangular or mummy-shaped coffin, often inscribed with magical texts and pictures of gods.

SCARAB: A desert beetle adopted by the Egyptians as the symbol of the sungod and creator of the universe.

SCRIBES: The educated professional class in Ancient Egypt. Scribes were responsible for carrying out the pharaoh's policies at all levels, and for documenting scientific knowledge.

VIZIER: An official second only to the king in importance and whose duties included the supervision of law-courts and the organization of the civil service.